Marriage of Christ

Brief quotes and references dealing with the plural marriage of Christ and his posterity:
1. Christ obtained a fulness of the priesthood by obtaining the fulness of the ordinances of the house of the Lord. This obviously, must include temple marriage. (1)
2. Jesus was married at the wedding of Cana of Galilee. (5,6,11,18,23)
3. There are individuals alive today who are descendants of the Savior and of the original Twelve apostles. (8,9,12,14,15,16,19)
4. Christ was a polygamist. (2,3,4,5,6,7,10,11)
5. According to the Prophet Joseph, the Savior received the fulness of the priesthood on the Mount of Transfiguration. In order for Christ to have received this he must have been married first.
6. See #24 for additional interesting thoughts from the Jewish viewpoint.

THE MARRIAGE OF CHRIST

1. *Teaching of the Prophet Joseph Smith, p. 308; June 11, 1843; Joseph Smith Jr.* If a man gets a fullness of the priesthood of God he has to get it in the same way that Jesus Christ obtained it, and that was by keeping all the commandments and obeying all the ordinances of the house of the Lord.

2. *J.D. 1:345-346; August 7, 1853; Salt Lake Tabernacle; Elder Jedediah M. Grant.* What does old Celsus say, who was a physician in the first century, whose medical worksare esteemed very highly at the present time. . . .He says, 'The grand reason why theGentiles and philosophers of his school persecuted Jesus Christ, was, because he had so many wives; there were Elizabeth, and Mary, and a host of others that followed him.' After Jesus went from the stage of action, the Apostles followed the example of their master. For instance, John the beloved disciple, writes in his second Epistle, 'Unto the elect lady and her children, whom I love in the truth.' Again, he says, 'Having many things to write unto you (or communicate), I would not write with paper and ink: but I trust to come unto you, and speak face to face, that our joy may be full.' Again--- 'The children of thy elect sister greet thee.' This ancient philosopher says they were both John's wives. Paul says, "Mine answer to them that do examine me is this:---Have we not power to lead about a sister, a wife, as well as other apostles, and as the brethren of the Lord, and Cephas." He, according to Celsus, had a numerous train of wives. The grand reason of the burst of public sentiment in anathemas upon Christ and his disciples, causing his crucifixion, was evidently based upon polygamy, according to the testimony of the philosophers who rose in that age. A belief in the doctrine of a plurality of wives caused the persecution of Jesus and his followers. We might almost think they were 'Mormons'.

3. *The Seer, pp. 159-160; October 1853; Elder Orson Pratt.* The Evangelists do not particularly speak of the marriage of Jesus; but this is not to be wondered at, for St. John says: 'There are also many other things which Jesus did, the which, if they should be written every one, I suppose that even the world itself could not contain the books that should be written.' (John 21:25) One thing is certain, that there were several holy women that greatly loved Jesus---such as Mary, and Martha her sister, and Mary Magdalene; and Jesus greatly loved them, and associated with them much; and when He arose from the dead, instead of first showing Himself to His chosen witnesses, the Apostles, He appeared first to these women, or at least to one of them---namely, Mary Magdalene. Now, it would be very natural for a husband in the resurrection to appear first to his own dear wives, and afterwards show himself to his other friends. If all the acts of Jesus were written, we no doubt should learn that these beloved women were his wives.

4. *The Seer, p. 172 Vol 1, No 11; November, 1853; Elder Orson Pratt.* From the passage in the forty-fifth Psalm, it will be seen that the great Messiah who was the founder of the Christian religion, was a Polygamist, as well as the Patriarch Jacob and the prophet David from whom He descended according to the flesh. Paul says concerning Jesus, "Verily he took not on him the nature of angels; but he took on him the seed of Abraham." (Heb. 2:16) Abraham the Polygamist, being a friend of God, the Messiah chose to take upon himself his seed; and by marrying many honorable wives himself, show to all future generations that he approbated the plurality of Wives under the Christian dispensation, as well as under the dispensations in which His Polygamist ancestors lived.

5. *J.D. 2:79-82; October 6, 1854; Pres. Orson Hyde; General Conference, S.L.C.* Our first parents, then, were commanded to multiply and replenish the earth; and if the Savior found it his duty to be baptized to fulfill all righteousness, a command of far less importance than that of multiplying his race, (if indeed there is any difference in the commandments of Jehovah, for they are all important, and all essential), would he not find it his duty to join in with the rest of the faithful ones in replenishing the earth? 'Mr. Hyde, do you really wish to imply that the immaculate Savior begat children? It is a blasphemous assertion against the purity of the Savior's life, to say the least of it. The holy aspirations that ever ascended from him to his Father would never allow him to have any such fleshly and carnal connexions, never, no never.' This is the general idea; but the Savior never thought it beneath him to obey the mandate of his Father; he never thought this stooping beneath his dignity; he never despised what God had made. . .'Then you really mean to hold to the doctrine that the Savior of the world was married; do you mean to be understood so? And if so, do you mean to be understood that he had more than one wife?' There is an old prophecy of Isaiah, which I cannot stop to read, but you will find it in the 53rd chapter of his prophecies; read the whole of the chapter. This particular prophecy speaks of Christ all the way through. It is there said, 'When thou shalt make his soul an offering for sin, he shall see his seed.' If he has no seed, how could he see them? How was it with Mary and Martha, and other women that followed him? In old times, and it is common in this day, the women, even as Sarah, called their husbands Lord; the word Lord is tantamount to husband in some languages, master, lord, husband, are about synonymous. In England we frequently hear the wife say, 'Where is my master?' She does not mean a tyrant, but as Sarah called her husband Lord, she designates hers by the word master. When Mary of old came to the sepulchre on the first day of the week, instead of finding Jesus she saw two angels in white, 'And they say unto her, Woman, why weepest thou? She said unto them, Because they have taken away my Lord,' or husband, 'and I know not where they have laid him. . . .Jesus saith unto her, Mary. She turned herself, and saith unto him, Rabboni; which is to say, Master.' Is there not here manifested the affections of a wife. These words speak the kindred ties and sympathies that are common to that relation of husband and wife. We will turn over to the account of the marriage in Cana of Galilee, and the mother of Jesus was there. Yes, and somebody else too. You will find it in the 2nd chapter of John's Gospel; remember it and read it when you go home. . . .Gentlemen, that is as plain as the translators, or different councils over this Scripture, dare allow it to go to the world, but the thing is there; it is told; Jesus was the bridegroom at the marriage of Cana of Galilee, and he told them what to do. Now there was actually a marriage; and if Jesus was not the bridegroom on that occasion, please tell who was. . . .I do not despise to be called a son of Abraham, if he had a dozen wives; or to be called a brother, a son, a child of the Savior, if he had Mary, and Martha, and several others, as wives; and though he did cast seven devils out of one of them, it is all the same to me. . . .Well, then, he shall see his seed, and who shall declare his generation, for he was cut off from the earth? I shall say here, that before the Savior died, he looked upon his own natural children, as we look upon ours; he saw his seed, and immediately afterwards he was cut off from the earth.

[Concerning the above talk, given here in part, Pres. Brigham Young said:] We have had a splendid address from brother Hyde, for which I am grateful. I feel in my heart to bless the people all the time, and can say amen to brother Hyde's remarks. . . .He has done so beautifully, and it will have its desired effect. (J.D. 2:90)

6. *J.D. 2:210; March 18, 1855; Salt Lake City; Pres. Orson Hyde.* I discover that some of the Eastern papers represent me as a great blasphemer, because I said, in my lecture on Marriage, at our last Conference, that Jesus Christ was married at Cana of Galilee, that Mary, Martha, and others were his wives, and that he begat children. All that I have to say in reply to that charge is this--- they worship a Savior that is too pure and holy to fulfill the commands of his Father. I worship one that is just pure and holy enough 'to fulfill all righteousness;' not only the righteous law of baptism, but the still more righteous and important law 'to multiply and replenish the earth.' Startle not at this! for even the Father himself honored that law by coming down to Mary, without a natural [mortal] body, and begetting a son; and if Jesus begat children, he only 'did that which he had seen his Father do.'

7. *Mary Ellen A. Kimball Journal; February 18, 1857; CHO.* [Heber C. Kimball] came to our room [and] said he did not feel well. spoke of an ordinance which he had previously taught and said that only one of his wives had attended to it. he then spoke of our Savior and his wives but more particularly of Mary [and her] faithfulness to her Lord.

8. *J.D. 4:248; March 1, 1857; Salt Lake Tabernacle; Pres. Heber C. Kimball.* What do you suppose we are going to do with you? Are you ever going to be prepared to see God, Jesus Christ, His angels, or comprehend His servants, unless you take a faithful and prayerful course? Did you actually know Joseph Smith? No. Do you know brother Brigham? No. Do you know brother Heber? No, you do not. Do you know the Twelve? You do not, if you did, you would begin to know God, and learn that those men who are chosen to direct and counsel you are near kindred to God and to Jesus Christ, for the keys, power, and authority of the kingdom of God are in that lineage. I speak of these things with a view to arouse your feelings and your faithfulness towards God the Father, and His Son Jesus Christ, that you may pray and be humble, and penitent.

9. *J.D. 4:259-260; March 1857; Salt Lake City; Pres. Orson Hyde.* It will be borne in mind that once on a time, there was a marriage in Cana of Galilee; and on a careful reading of that transaction, it will be discovered that no less a person than Jesus Christ was married on that occasion. If he was never married, his intimacy with Mary and Martha, and the other Mary also whom Jesus loved, must have been highly unbecoming and improper to say the best of it. . . .Did Christ come to destroy the law of the Prophets, or to fulfill them? He came to fulfill. Did he multiply, and did he see his seed: Did he honour his Father's law by complying with it, or did he not? Others may do as they like, but I will not charge our Savior with neglect or transgression in this or any other duty. . . .If God be not our Father, grandfather, or great grandfather, or some kind of a father in reality, in deed and in truth, why are we taught to say, 'Our Father who art in heaven?' How much soever of holy horror this doctrine may excite in persons not impregnated with the blood of Christ, and whose minds are consequently dark and benighted, it may excite still more when they are told that if none of the natural blood of Christ flows in their veins, they are not the chosen or elect of God. Object not, therefore, too strongly against the marriage of Christ, but remember that in the last days, secret and hidden things must come to light, and that your life also (which is the blood) is hid with Christ in God.

10. *J.D. 11:328; February 10, 1867; Salt Lake Tabernacle; Pres. Brigham Young.* Yet the whole fraternity [of Freemasonry] throughout Christendom will cry out against this order [of polygamy]. "Oh dear, oh dear, oh dear!" What is the matter? "I am in pain," they all cry out, "I am suffering at witnessing the wickedness there

is in our land. Here is one of the 'relics of barbarism!' " Yes, one of the relics of Adam, of Enoch, of Noah, of Abraham, of Isaac, of Jacob, of Moses, David, Solomon, the Prophets, of Jesus, and his Apostles.

11. *Journal of Wilford Woodruff; July 22, 1883.* Joseph F. Smith . . . spoke upon the marriage in Cana of Galilee. He thought Jesus was the bridegroom and Mary and Martha the brides. He also referred to Luke 10th chap., 34 to 42 verses. Also John 11th chap., 2 & 5 verses, John 12:13. Joseph Smith spoke upon these passages to show that Mary and Martha manifested much closer relationship than merely a believer.

12. *Journal of Oliver B. Huntington; Wednesday, December 29, 1886.* While visiting with Zina [Huntington] she related a conversation that occurred between her and a sister "Repshere" upon events in Nauvoo, where the Prophet Joseph Smith sealed her, Sister Repshere, to a Judge Adams of Springfield, Illinois.

The Prophet stated to her [Repshere] that Judge Adams was a literal descendant of Jesus Christ. The Judge died in Nauvoo and Sister Repshere, his wife, who had been married before to [a Mr.] Repshere, died at Hill Creek, Utah.

[NOTE: Judge Adams was a very close friend of the Prophet Joseph. He was one of the original nine men who received the endowment when it was first given on the 4th of May, 1842. Before Judge Adams death, Joseph said he anointed him to the Patriarchal power, and that he [Adams] had had revelations concerning his departure. The Prophet Joseph spoke at his funeral.]

13. *First Presidency Letterpress Copybooks; 1877-1949, pp. 286-288; CR/1/20/#19 June 10, 1890.* [Geo. Reynolds gives a few reasons why he believed Jesus was married. Among his remarks was the following as a proof as to Christ's marriage:]
June 10, 1890
Margaret M. Parsons:
Dear Sister:
". . . . Again recollect the supper at the house of Simon the leaper, when Mary, in her great affliction, anointed the feet of the Savior. . . ."

14. *Solemn Assembly Minutes, Salt Lake Temple; Sunday, 2 July, 1899.* President George Q. Cannon also spoke on the law of tithing. Among other things, said, "There are those in this audience who are descendants of the old Twelve Apostles - and, shall I say it, yes, descendants of the Savior himself. His seed is represented in this body of men."

15. *Journal of Rudger Clawson, pp. 374-375; President of the Quorum of the Twelve.* Minutes of a solemn assembly meeting Sunday, July 2, 1899, Salt Lake Temple.

President George Q. Cannon also spoke on the law of tithing. Among other things he said, "There are those in this audience who are descendants of the Twelve Apostles--and shall I say it, yes, Descendants of the Savior himself. His seed is represented in this body of men."

Following President Cannon, President Snow arose and said that what Brother Cannon had stated respecting the literal descendants among this company of the old apostles and the Savior himself is true--that the Savior's seed is represented in this body of men.

16. *Journal of Anthony W. Ivins. Minutes of a Solemn Assembly in the Salt Lake Temple, Sunday, July 2, 1899.* George Q. Cannon. There are men in this congregation who are descendants of the ancient Twelve Apostles, and I shall say it, of the Son of God himself, for he had seed, and in time they shall be known.

17. *Millennial Star Vol 62:97; President Joseph F. Smith; 1900.* Jesus Christ never omitted the fulfilling of a single law that God has made known for the salvation of the children of men. It would not have done for him to have come and obeyed one law and neglected another. He could not consistently do that and then say to mankind, 'Follow me.'

18. *Jesus the Christ, p. 155; 1915 ed.; James E. Talmage.* She manifested concern and personal responsibility in the matter of providing for the guests. Evidently her position was different from that of one present by ordinary invitation. Whether this circumstance indicates the marriage to have been that of one of her own immediate family, or some more distant relative, we are not informed [by John's gospel].

19. *Life of Heber C. Kimball, p. 185; Copyright 1955; Elder Orson F. Whitney.* His [Heber's], also, was of the Savior's lineage; in his heart a kindred spirit, in his veins the self-same blood.

20. *The Gospel According to Thomas, p. 57; Translated from the Coptic Text, 1962.* . . . .They [the disciples] said to Him: Shall we then, being children, enter the Kingdom? Jesus said to them: When you make the two one, (one flesh--or marriage) and when you make the inner as the outer. . .and when you make the male and the female into a single one, (married), so that the male will not be male and female (not) be female, . . .then shall you enter (the Kingdom). Simon Peter said to them? Let Mary go out from among us, because women are not worthy of the Life. Jesus said: See, I shall lead her, so that I will make her male, (one in marriage) that she too may become a living spirit, resembling you males. For every woman who makes herself male will enter the Kingdom of Heaven.

21. *The Gospel of Philip, pp. 96-97, 115; Translated from the Coptic Text by R. McL. Wilson; BYU/#229.8/P537/e. (c) 1962.* There were three who walked with the Lord at all times, Mary (his mother), and her sister, and Magdalene, whom they called his consort. . . .And the consort of Christ is Mary Magdalene. The Lord loved Mary more than all the disciples, and kissed her on her mouth often. The others too (the disciples) . . . .they said to him 'Why do you love her more than all of us?' The Saviour answered and said to them 'Why do I not love you like her?' [End of Translation]

22. *Letter from Pres. David O. McKay; October 10, 1966.* I have been directed to tell you that there is no scripture or revelation on this subject [Christ being married]. The wisest presumption upon this and related subjects mentioned in your letter is that the status of Christ, a member of the Godhead, so far transcends the status of human beings and what they can attain in a life-time of utter and complete faithfulness and perfection, that we should suspend and defer all concern about His status.

23. Doc New Testament Commentary 1:135; 1973 edition; Elder Bruce R. McConkie. John's record of the marriage in Cana is fragmentary; it does not by any means tell the whole story. From what is recorded, however, we learn:
 (1) Mary seemed to be the hostess at the marriage party, the one in charge, the one responsible for the entertainment of the guests. It was she who recognized the need for more wine, who sought to replenish the supply, who directed the servants to follow whatever instructions Jesus gave. Considering the customs of the day, it is a virtual certainty that one of Mary's children was being married.

24. Interesting Thoughts:
    1. The Jews were all married by age 20. Those who were not married were forced by the civil courts to marry. Celibacy was not known to them.

2. All those who were "rabbis" were married, and Christ was called a "rabbi" on many occasions: Mark 9:5; 11:21; Matt 26:25, 49; John 1:49, 38; 4:31; 9:2; 11:8; 6:25.
3. Although Christ spoke out against adultery, he did not say anything against plural marriage.
4. Plural marriage among the Jews was still the custom in the days of the Savior.
5. Failure to marry was considered a sin among the Jews.
6. The word "woman" in Greek translations means "wife".
7. The term "master" in the Greek means "husband".
8. The term "consort" means husband or wife.
9. The first commandment to have children was to obeyed by all Jews.
10. Jesus was "called" to the wedding of Cana. Jewish tradition "calls" the bridegroom to the wedding.
11. At Jewish weddings the bridegroom is the one who is to handle the refreshments or wine.
12. Only immediate family members are allowed to anoint the bodies of their dead.
13. Christ first appeared to Mary after his resurrection.
14. Christ said to Mary: "Hold me not", not "Touch me not".
15. Christ was intimate with Mary and Martha, they washed his feet and anointed his body, etc.
16. Did Christ set the example in all things for us to follow?
17. Would Christ want his marriage to be performed for him by proxy?
18. How would Christ know the problems or joys of marriage had he not experienced them?

Journal of Rudger Clawson
President of the Quorum of the Twelve
Typescript of minutes of a solemn assembly held in the Salt Lake Temple, Sunday, July 2, 1899
pp 374-375

This being the day for the Solemn Assembly called by the First Presidency, a large number of brethren were admitted to the temple at 10 o'clock and were seated in the Celestial and Terrestrial rooms.

There were about 700 present, as follows, The First Presidency, the Twelve, First Seven Presidents of Seventies, Presiding Patriarch, Presiding Bishopric, Presidencies of Stakes, the Bishops of Wards, Stake Presidencies of YMMIA, Relief Societies, Sunday Schools and others.

Meeting was called to order by President Lorenzo Snow. Singing by the Temple Choir: prayer by Apostle F. M. Lyman. Singing.

President Snow said that if the brethren present lived ten, fifteen, or twenty years, or perhaps less, they would go back to Jackson County. The time for returning to Jackson County is much nearer than many suppose and it is the faithful that would be selected to go, and they will be required to accept the United Order. Read of the troubles and curses that are visited upon apostates, said he would tell us what the Lord required of us today. Read Section 119 of the Doctrine and Covenants. Talked upon the subject of tithing. If the people, he said, had paid an honest tithing for the past year we would have received $1,000,000 more than we did receive, and if full tithing had been paid for the past twelve years, we would have received 10,000,000 $ more than we did receive.

Bishop Preston says, and the books prove it, that only about 50 percent tithing is paid. A half tithing or a third tithing is no tithing at all, but simply an offering. If we do not observe this law we have no promise that we shall remain in this land an hour. Said that while visiting in St. George on his recent trip the Lord revealed to him that counsel he should impart to the people, and the word of the Lord was that the Saints should pay their tithing. Trouble has come upon the people. In the south stock is dying off, crops are drying up, and the north crops were partially destroyed by frost. An effort is being made to influence the Government to disfranchise the Latter-day Saints by an constitutional amendment. How far this is due to the disobedience of our people in observing the law of tithing I do not know, but the Saints are certainly under condemnation.

Bishop Preston followed, So far as he could ascertain, he said, there is about one-fourth of the Saints that pay no tithing at all, while the average tithing paid by those who pay is not more than fifty percent, and may fall below that average.

Song. Sacrament.

President Snow read Section 86, Doctrine and Covenants. Said we are the sons and daughters of the Lord, and descendants of the prophets and apostles. Said the Lord has forgiven us for our carelessness in paying our tithing in the past, but he will forgive us no longer, and if we do not obey this law, we will be scattered as were the Saints in Jackson County, and this by reason of the knowledge we have attained to. What I say is as true as God lives. We must teach the people this law of tithing--first by paying tithes ourselves. Just as sure as we live, if we do not honor the law of tithing, we will never possess the land of Jackson County, except it be by the shedding of blood, but it will not be by the shedding of blood because you will listen to my voice, and the voice of my brethren.

We are the sons of the prophets and the sons of God. The Lord will not send hornets to drive the people out of Jackson County, as he promised to drive the people out of the land of promise before the children of Israel, but he will send cyclones, earthquakes, and pestilences.

Apostle M. F. Cowley made brief remarks upon the law of tithing.

Recess. Lunch was served in the assembly room on the upper floor. Had sandwiches, cheese, buns and cakes. In view of the long fast, the lunch seemed to be greatly relished by all.

About 5 o'clock, meeting was resumed in the Celestial and Terrestrial rooms. Singing. Instructive remarks were made by the brethren upon the law of tithing: LeRoi Snow, Apostles George Teasdale and President Joseph F. Smith. The latter, in speaking of tithing, said the books should not only record what we do, but what we ought to have done, and did not do. A man is in poor business as President or Bishop of a Ward who says to the people, "Do as you ought to do, not as I do." The poor of a ward --the widows and orphans all should pay their tithing.

President George Q. Cannon also spoke on the law of tithing. Among other things he said, "There are those in this audience who are descendants of the Twelve Apostles--and shall I say it, yes, Descendants of the Savior himself. His seed is represented in this body of men."

Following President Cannon, President Snow arose and said that what Brother Cannon had stated respecting the literal descendants among this company of the old apostles and the Savior himself is true--that the Savior's seed is represented in this body of men. President Snow further said in conclusion he hoped the brethren would take the spirit of these meetings home with them and impart the same to the people.

A resolution to the effect that the brethren would accept the law of tithing, obey it themselves and teach it to the people was adopted by a rising vote and with uplifted hands.

President Snow then led in the sacred shout, and the meeting came to a close. Singing. Benediction by Seymour B Young.

THE MARRIAGE RELATIONS.

A Lecture by President Orson Hyde, delivered at the General Conference, in the Tabernacle, Great Salt Lake City, October 6, 1854.

Beloved Friends and Brethren--It appears to have fallen to my lot to be your speaker at this time, and to call your attention to a subject that was proposed in the former part of the day.

At the time I gave out the appointment for this evening's meeting, my eye was fixed upon another person to deliver the lecture. I shall try to do the subject as good justice as my abilities, aided by the faith of the Saints and the Spirit of God, may enable me to do. I desire not only your candid and undivided attention, but I trust I shall also have your prayers, that the Lord may inspire me with those arguments and reasons that are well pleasing in His sight, that I may acquit myself before Him, if it may not be my good fortune to acquit myself so amply before you as my heart would desire.

While reflecting upon the subject of this evening's lecture, those words occurred to my mind, which our Savior spake to the Jews, who considered themselves righteous, and looked upon others with distrust and disdain--in short, who looked upon others as sinners; to reprove them, he said, "Ye are they which justify yourselves before men; but God knoweth your hearts: for that which is highly esteemed among men is abomination in the sight of God."

I do not know that I shall confine myself to this text particularly. Although I have repeated these words for the text, yet the text is not a guide at all times for the servant of God. It is the letter that killeth, we read, but it is the Spirit that giveth life. The Spirit of the Almighty is the agent by which His servants should ever be led.

The words contained in this Bible are merely a history of what is gone by; it was never given to guide the servant of God in the course he should pursue, any more than the words and commandments of God, given to a generation under one set of circumstances, would serve for another generation under another set of circumstances. There must be something to suggest or to draw forth the command to answer the circumstance under which we are placed at the time.

It is so with the servants of God. There is a Spirit that is ever ready, and points out, under varied and conflicting circumstances, the very course which the servants of God should pursue. The Bible is not a sufficient guide; it is only the history of the people who lived 1800 years ago. The history of our Church in this day, presents the scenes and transactions of this people--the revelations and words of God to them; but if an individual living an hundred, or eighteen hundred, years hence, under different circumstances, were to adopt the history of this people for his guide in all things, he would not find it sufficient to answer the circumstances surrounding him.

Hence, it is the letter that killeth, and the Spirit giveth life. In the light of that celestial agent I ever hope to walk. I hope that it may be not only my helm and guide, but yours also, through all the labyrinths and windings of this mortal life, until we attain a standing upon ground celestial.

I have heard it remarked sometimes, by individuals who were not identified or connected with our Church, that if they could only be convinced that polygamy was true, they would become "Mormons" at once.

Do you believe the Bible? "Certainly I do," says the inquirer. Did father Abraham and the ancient Patriarchs live in this relation, and practise this doctrine? You say they did. Then if what they practised is true, you are bound to become a "Mormon," upon your own hypothesis and reasons. But, gentlemen, if I know that that was the all-convincing argument, and if that was the principal doctrine that alone influenced you to become a "Mormon," I should at once say, let me never baptize such a person, let me never be the agent to bring such a person into the Church and kingdom of God.

God despises every character who would enter His Church for no other purpose than to criminally indulge his natural propensities. Then, gentlemen, do not indulge the expectation, if you should be convinced by the arguments I may adduce in favor of the doctrine of polygamy, as it is called, that that will prove a sufficient groundwork for your faith. But where is the ground upon which to base your faith? Where shall you go to find out "Mormonism" from the foundation to the top-stone, from the root to the uttermost branch in the tree? Begin at the beginning. If men wish to accomplish any work, they must begin at the beginning of that work, not in the middle of it, or at the end. I must begin at the beginning, and I know that the first stone is laid upon a permanent foundation, I can then with safety add another to that already laid; but if I cannot lay the first stone upon the ground that is solid--if I cannot lay it upon a rock, I may despair of ever rearing a fabric or superstructure that will resist the rain and winds that may be hurled against it by the power of nature. We must begin at the beginning, and not content ourselves by grasping at that which may be beautiful in illustration and enlist our attention, and begin to build upon it as a foundation. In such a case we may have branches, but we do not bear the root.

I know that this doctrine is made the subject of a great deal of ridicule. I know that the world at large who profess to be pious, or, if not pious, morally upright, look upon it as a damning sin, as a stain upon the bright escutcheon of their country, here in the very heart of the United States territory, surrounded by tall mountains; they consider it a dark spot in the country's history. Many of the great politicians of the day view it in this point of light. Religionists are still more scrupulous--they regard it as a heinous and damning sin.

I always consider it my duty, under proper circumstances, to give a reason of the hope that is in me, with meekness and fear; and if I have imbibed a principle, and am unable to defend it upon the principles of truth, justice, equity, and true philosophy, I should consider I was walking in the dark.

Whenever truth is manifested by revelation to the servants of God, it never comes without a reason for it. When the light of revelation bursts upon the mind, it not only unfolds one principle, but many. For instance, to illustrate this idea, suppose this room were in total darkness, and we were seated as we now are, if a brilliant light were introduced in the midst of the room, it would enable us to see not only one person, but the whole multitude.

So it is with the light of revelation. When it bursts into the human mind, it not only reveals one principle, but casts a halo of light upon all connected with it. An individual thus favored, walks in the light of Jehovah's countenance. I have a desire that in this light we may walk; and he whose eye is single, says the Savior, his whole body shall be full of light, and there is no darkness in him, nor occasion of stumbling.

What is the condition of the world at large, both religious and political, who regard us as being in the depths of sin, iniquity, and transgression? What are their customs? Go, if you please, to the large cities of every nation and clime. I have visited many of them in the four quarters of the earth, and in the islands of the sea. I have had some little experience in relation to these things, so far as common observation could give it to me, and I pretty well understand the manner of life of the world at large.

A man, for instance, who has the most riches, the man who can command the most wealth, I do not say this is the case with all, but it is the case with the majority---they not only have their wives and families with whom they publicly live and associate, but they also have in secret places their mistresses, whom they maintain not honorably, but under a cloak as it were. When by their illegitimate connexions they are likely to increase their race, what means do they resort to, to save their credit, to keep their honor unsullied in the eyes of the multitude, to cover up their iniquity, hide their crimes, and smother their shame? A skilful practitioner is employed to destroy the embryo offspring. This is murder.

Nor is this the only means used to hide their shame, and save themselves from reproach. They may be successful in hiding their iniquity from the eye of man, but they cannot hide from the eye of the Omnipotent Jehohovah [sic]. Is there not a day coming when these acts will be searched out, and proclaimed abroad, and that, too, by a mind that penetrates the secret thoughts and intents of the hearts of the children of men? "What! is there indeed such a day approaching?" Yes. It may be hid for a little season from the view of the wicked, but it is steadily approaching, and will come as a thief in the night; and those very persons, both male and female, who often throw out their anathemas against the "Mormons," against their course, and manner of life, will be overwhelmed with it.

Then how will apply the words of our text--"Ye are they that justify yourselves before men, but God knoweth your hearts; for that which is well pleasing in the sight of men, is an abomination to God." What is well pleasing in the eyes of worldly men--men devoid of principle, and destitute of the righteousness of God? It is pleasing to them to hide and smother up anything that would tend to cast reproach and infamy upon their name. The blackness of their character they seek to conceal from the public gaze, and appear good Christians, and honorable men in society, men of principle, virtue, and integrity. If they can hide their shame, no matter what the expense or suffering caused in destroying the embryo coming into being. They care not to risk the life of her who would become a mother. All this is well pleasing in the eyes of unprincipled men, and that their iniquity should not come to light.

But that that is well pleasing in the sight of men, is an abomination in the sight of God. I will venture to say, that you may go into the most populous cities of the world, and you will find a considerable part of those who give tone to Christianity as it is in the world, standing in these miserable relations, under cover, and in secret. These things are true, and it is enough to pain the heart of the philanthropist, and wound the feeling of any man who is the friend of suffering humanity, to read their history, and observe their course. I would not follow them in all their filthy windings, were I able. Had I the discerning eye of an angel, or of a God, I would not wish to follow them up, and disclose to you the corruptions that are practised in the world, and all under the cloak of popularity, shrouded by high standing, and worldly authority; and thus they are protected in their unlawful relations.

I am not disposed to charge home upon the lawgivers of our country things of this kind; I will not presume to do it; yet at the same time, if I can credit their own statements in relation to the acts of one another touching these matters, it is enough to make the nations blush and hide their heads in shame, from such miserable, MISERABLE, corrupt proceedings.

But we do not wish to sustain our own position upon the corruptions of others--our own position, as it is in the mind and revelations of God. God forbid that our faith should be founded upon the corruptions of the world. Our faith is founded upon the purity of the word of life and there let it be grounded.

Well, now, friends and brethren, will you listen to me for a short time, and let me conduct you as far as I shall be able this evening, through the volume of inspiration that is universally acknowledged by all Christendom to be the word of God, the truth of heaven? Will you listen to some of the sayings contained in that book? And then say whether we possess the same spirit now that inspired the breasts of the ancients, whose history is penned upon these pages. Judge for yourselves whether it be so or not.

In the first place, then, we will look unto Abraham our father, and to Sarah who bore us, for if we are Christ's, then we are Abraham's seed, and heirs according to the promise. Let any story be told of my father whereby dishonor is laid to his charge, or let any reproach be cast upon my mother, and if the feelings of the loyalty of a son towards his parents dwell in my bosom I will resist all such reproach. No matter how sinful they might have been, their sins must not be portrayed before me. I look then unto Abraham as my father, and unto Sarah as my mother who bore me. How was it, then, with Abraham? He is said to be the father of the faithful, and the great head of the Church in the days of the Patriarchs, and the head of those who have been adopted into the covenant of Jehovah through the blood of His only begotten; for if we are Christ's then we are Abraham's seed, and heirs according to the promise. If, by the virtue of the Savior's blood, our sins are washed away, we are the children of Abraham; we hail him as our father, and Sarah as our mother; he is the father of the faithful, he is the father of many nations. How was it with Abraham? Did he please God, walk before Him uprightly, and obtain this testimony that he pleased God, and obtain promises that no other man has obtained since the days of Abraham, the Son of God excepted? Jehovah promised that in him and in his seed all the nations of the earth should be blessed, as a pattern of piety, and as the great head of the Church. Because of his faithfulness in keeping the commandments of Jehovah on earth, he drew from on high this great promise. Who has lived since that time who has been thus blessed? I will venture to say not one. Then if we are his children, will we not do the works of faithful Abraham? So said the Savior, who ever spoke the truth, who ever declared the mind and will of his Father in heaven. Are we Abraham's seed, or are we bastards and not sons? That is the question.

Let us see what Abraham's works were. Abraham obtained promises. What promise have you obtained? What promise has the Christian world obtained? "Why," says one, "the Bible is all full of promises made to the people of God long ago." But what have the promises to the people of God long ago to do with us? Have we obtained promises to ourselves? There is the point. If our fathers obtained promises that they should be fed, and were fed, their eating and drinking does not satisfy my appetite. It satisfied them, but that has nothing to do with me, I want the same kind of substantial food myself. If Abraham obtained promises, I want to obtain promises also. "What! A man that has more than one wife obtain promises from God?" I tell you there were but few in olden times who ever did obtain promises from God, that had not more than one wife, if the Bible be true. There was David, and there was Solomon; there were the whole line of the kings of Israel. Says one, "That Old Bible was for the Jews, and has nothing to do with us; that is the Old Testament; and having more wives was according to their law, and according to their custom, but it does not apply to us; the Savior of the world is our great pattern, he is our great lawgiver."

And how is it with him? Let us Inquire. Did the Savior of the world consider it to be his duty to fulfill righteousness? You answer, yes. Even the simple ordinance of baptism he would not pass by, for the Lord commanded it, and therefore it was righteousness to obey what the Lord had commanded, and he would fulfil all righteousness. Upon this hypothesis I will go back to the beginning, and notice the commandment that was given to our first parents in the garden of Eden. The Lord said unto them, "Multiply and replenish the earth." I will digress here for a moment from the thread of the subject, and bring an idea that may perhaps have a bearing upon it.

The earth, you remember, was void and empty, until our first parents began at the garden of Eden. What does the term replenish mean? This word is derived from the Latin; "re" and "plenus;" "re" denotes repetition, iteration; and "plenus" signifies full, complete; then the meaning of the word replenish is, to refill, recomplete. If I were to go into a merchant's store, and find he had got a new stock of goods, I should say--"You have replenished your stock, that is, filled up your establishment, for it looks as it did before." "Now go forth," says the Lord, "and replenish the earth;" for it was covered with gloomy clouds of darkness, excluded from the light of heaven, and darkness brooded upon the face of the deep. The world was peopled before the days of Adam, as much so as it was before the days of Noah. It was said that Noah became the father of a new world, but it was the same old world still, and will continue to be, though it may pass through many changes.

When God said, Go forth and replenish the earth; it was to replenish the inhabitants of the human species, and make it as it was before. Our first parents, then, were commanded to multiply and replenish the earth; and if the Savior found it his duty to be baptized to fulfil all righteousness, a command of far less importance than that of multiplying his race, (if indeed there is any difference in the commandments of Jehovah, for they are all important, and all essential,) would he not find it his duty to join in with the rest of the faithful ones in replenishing the earth? "Mr. Hyde, do you really wish to imply that the immaculate Savior begat children? It is a blasphemous assertion against the purity of the Savior's life, to say the least of it. The holy aspirations that ever ascended from him to his Father would never allow him to have any such fleshly and carnal connexions, never, no never." This is the general idea; but the Savior never thought it beneath him to obey the mandate of his Father; he never thought this stooping beneath his dignity; he never despised what God had made; for they are bone of his bone, and flesh of his flesh; kindred spirits, that once basked in rays of immortality and eternal life. When he found them clothed upon and surrounded with the weaknesses of mortal flesh, would he despise them? No. It is true, I have seen men who became poor and miserable all at once, and then those who were their friends in the days of their prosperity turn from them, and scarcely deign to bestow them a look, it being too humiliating to associate with them in their poverty. But it was not so with the Savior; he associated with them in other spheres, and when they came here, descending below all things, he did not despise to associate with these same kindred spirits. "Then you really mean to hold to the doctrine that the Savior of the world was married; do you mean to be understood so? And if so, do you mean to be understood that he had more than one wife?"

The Christian world by their prejudices have driven us away from the Old Bible, so we must now appeal to the New Testament, for that seems to suit the prejudice of the people; though to me it is all alike, both the Old and New Testaments; for the scribe that is well instructed, brings out of his treasury things both new and old. This is my treasury, or rather, it is one of my treasuries, and what I cannot find there, I trust will come down from on high, and lodge in my heart. The gift of God is also my treasury, even the Holy Spirit.

Now suppose I should set out myself, and travel through the cities of the nation as a celebrated reformer, preaching revelations and sentiments as lofty as the skies, and rolling out ideas strange and new, to which the multitude were entirely unaccustomed; and wherever I went, suppose I had with me three or four women--one combing my head, another washing my feet, and another shedding tears upon them, and wiping them with the hair of her head. Suppose I should lean upon them, and they upon me, would it not appear monstrous in the eyes of the world? Would they ride me into Jerusalem upon our ass's colt, and cast branches of the palm tree beneath my feet, shouting, "Hosannah, blessed is he that cometh in the name of the Lord, hosannah in the highest?" I guess they would give me a coat of tar and feathers, and ride me on a rail; and it is my opinion they would serve the Savior the same, did he go about now as he did eighteen hundred years ago.

There is an old prophecy of Isaiah, which I cannot stop to read, but you will find it in the 53rd chapter of his prophecies; read the whole of the chapter. This particular prophecy speaks of Christ all the way through. It is there said, "When thou shalt make his soul an offering for sin, he shall see his seed." What constitutes the soul? The spirit and body of man united; for you know it is said in one place that so many souls were slain in the night by the angel of God. The immortal part was not slain, but a disunion of the mortal and immortal parts took place. When they shall make his soul an offering for sin, he shall see his seed. If he has no seed, how could he see them? When they make his soul an offering for sin, he shall see his seed, and prolong his days, and the pleasure of the Lord shall prosper in his hand." By and bye the Prophet goes on to say, "And who shall declare his generation," for his life is taken from the earth. If he had no generation, who could declare it. I told you there was an agent who would bring out every subject in bold relief, which is the Holy Ghost, who searcheth all things, even the deep things of God, and until that celestial agent should fire some man's heart to declare his generation, it could never be made known. Who shall declare it? He could not, for he was cut off from the earth. I have noticed the prophecy of Isaiah, that portion of it which was fulfilled in the person of the Savior, for the Lord divided him a portion with the great, "and he shall divide the spoil with the strong; because he hath poured out his soul unto death: and he was numbered with the transgressors; and he bare the sin of many, and made intercession for the transgressors." Upon him was laid the iniquity of us all; he was numbered with thieves, and in his expiring moments he said, "Father, forgive them; for they know not what they do." "He was oppressed, and he was afflicted, yet he opened not his mouth; he is brought as a lamb to the slaughter, and as a sheep before her shearers is dumb, so he openeth not his mouth. He was taken from prison and from judgment: and who shall declare his generation? for he was cut off out of the land of the living: for the transgression of my people was he stricken." Now if one portion of this prophecy has been fulfilled, the other portion has, or will be.

How was it with Mary and Martha, and other women that followed him? In old times, and it is common in this day, the women, even as Sarah, called their husbands Lord; the word Lord is tantamount to husband in some languages, master, lord, husband, are about synonymous. In England we frequently hear the wife say, "Where is my master?" She does not mean a tyrant, but as Sarah called her husband Lord, she designates hers by the word master. When Mary of old came to the sepulchre on the first day of the week, instead of finding Jesus she saw two angels in white, "And they say unto her, Woman, why weepest thou? She said unto them, Because they have taken away my Lord," or husband, "and I know not where they have laid him. And when she had thus said, she turned herself back, and saw Jesus standing, and knew not that it was Jesus. Jesus saith unto her, Woman, why weepest thou? whom seekest thou? She, supposing him to be the gardener, saith unto him, Sir, if thou have borne him hence, tell me where thou hast laid him, and I will take him away. Jesus saith unto her, Mary. She turned herself, and saith unto him, Rabboni; which is to say, Master." Is there not here manifested the affections of a wife. These words speak the kindred ties and sympathies that are common to that relation of husband and wife. Where will you find a family so nearly allied by the ties of common religion? "Well," you say, "that appears rather plausible, but I want a little more evidence, I want you to find where it says the Savior was actually married."

Have you ever read your Bibles? I must confess I have not read it for some time, but looked more to Him who rules on high, and to those who hold the words of life in the inspiration of the Holy Ghost; I look to them more frequently than to it. I have once memorized the Bible, and when any one quoted one verse, I could quote the next. I have memorized it in English, German, and Hebrew, still I do not profess to be very familiar with it now, yet the sentiments and spirit of it are in my heart, and will be as long as I live, and still remain when I am gone to another sphere. When does it say the Savior was married? I believe I will read it for your accommodation, or you might not believe my words were I to say that there is indeed such a Scripture.

We will turn over to the account of the marriage in Cana of Galilee, and the mother of Jesus was there. Yes, and somebody else too. You will find it in the 2nd chapter of John's Gospel; remember it and read it when you go home. "And the third day there was a marriage in Cana of Galilee; and the mother of Jesus was there: and both Jesus was called, and his disciples, to the marriage. And when they wanted wine, the mother of Jesus saith unto him, They have no wine. Jesus saith unto her, Woman, what have I to do with thee? mine hour is not yet come. His mother saith unto the servants, Whatsoever he saith unto you, do it. And there were set there six water pots of stone, after the manner of the purifying of the Jews, containing two or three firkins apiece. Jesus saith unto them, Fill the water pots with water. And they filled them up to the brim. And he saith unto them, Draw out now, and bear unto the governor of the feast. And they bare it. When the ruler of the feast had tasted the water that was made wine, and knew not whence it was: (but the servants which drew the water knew;) the governor of the feast called the bridegroom, and saith unto him"--that is, the ruler of the feast saith unto the bridegroom, "Every man at the beginning doth set forth good wine; and when men have well drunk, then that which is worse: but thou hast kept the good wine until now."

Gentlemen, that is as plain as the translators, or different councils over this Scripture, dare allow it to go to the world, but the thing is there; it is told; Jesus was the bridegroom at the marriage of Cana of Galilee, and he told them what to do.

Now there was actually a marriage; and if Jesus was not the bridegroom on that occasion, please tell who was. If any man can show this, and prove that it was not the Savior of the world, then I will acknowledge I am in error. We say it was Jesus Christ who was married, to be brought into the relation whereby he could see his seed, before he was crucified. "Has he indeed passed by the nature of angels, and taken upon himself the seed of Abraham, to die without leaving a seed to bear his name on the earth?" No. But when the secret is fully out, the seed of the blessed shall be gathered in, in the last days; and he who has not the blood of Abraham flowing in his veins, who has not one particle of the Savior's in him, I am afraid is a stereotyped Gentile, who will be left out and not be gathered in the last days; for I tell you it is the chosen of God, the seed of the blessed, that shall be gathered. I do not despise to be called a son of Abraham, if he had a dozen wives; or to be called a brother, a son, a child of the Savior, if he had Mary, and Martha, and several others, as wives; and though he did cast seven devils out of one of them, it is all the same to me.

Well, then, he shall see his seed, and who shall declare his generation, for he was cut off from the earth? I shall say here, that before the Savior died, he looked upon his own natural children, as we look upon ours; he saw his seed, and immediately afterwards he was cut off from the earth; but who shall declare his generation? They had no father to hold them in honorable remembrance; they passed into the shades of obscurity, never to be exposed to mortal eye as the seed of the blessed one. For no doubt had they been exposed to the eye of the world, those infants might have shared the same fate as the children of Jerusalem in the days of Herod, when all the children were ordered to be slain under such an age, with the hopes of slaying the infant Savior. They might have suffered by the hand of the assassin, as the sons of many kings have done who were heirs apparent to the thrones of their fathers.

History is replete with circumstances of neck-or-nothing politicians dyeing their hands in the blood of those who stood in their way to the throne or to power.

That seed has had its influence upon the chosen of God in the last days. The same spirit inspires them that inspires their father, who bled and died upon the cross after the manner of the flesh.

Well, but, says one, there was certainly an injunction laid upon the Bishops in New Testament times, that they should have but one wife. This is brought up as a great argument against the position the Latter-day Saints have taken. In olden times they might have passed through the same circumstances as some of the Latter-day Saints had to in Illinois. What would it have done for us, if they had known that many of us had more than one wife when we lived in Illinois? They would have broken us up, doubtless, worse than they did. They may break us up, and rout us from one place to another, but by and bye we shall come to a point where we shall have all the women, and they will have none. You may think I am joking about this, but I can bring you the truth of God to demonstrate it to you. I have not advanced anything I have not got an abundance of backing for. There is more truth than poetry in this as sure as you live.

The Bishops anciently, in their office and callings, had a great deal to do with temporal matters--serving tables, attending to the poor, &c. And in as much as so much trust was reposed in them of a temporal character, the were required to have a fair reputation, and must not stand in any relation that would in the least prejudice their reputation with the world of mankind.

In certain countries, plurality of wives is legal. Christendom think they are about everybody, and the "rest of mankind" are few and far between. I have travelled among nations and countries where this doctrine was tolerated by law, and I will venture to say, if we were to take a walk through the world to-night, and find out those who are in favor of, or against, this doctrine, the majority would be in its favor. Could the whole world be assembled here before me, and a vote taken upon this subject, they would give us the right of conscience in this matter.

Has not the Mahomedan a right to be in favor of it? Did not God make him? And is not his right as dear to him as ours? Why should we set ourselves up as a little family of nations in Christendom, and say to the rest of the great family of the world, "You shall not do so and so, and you shall do this or that?" Why should we be restricted in this matter, while the great majority of the world decide in its favor?

Take this question up upon political principles, and what do the majority of the world say about it? They establish our right. Then take it upon the principles of natural philosophy, and the truth of our position is made still more apparent. Had I language to portray to the most delicate ear the principles of our existence, and the laws of our nature, the most stubborn sceptic would be obliged to yield to the power of truth. I might take up the subject in this point of light, but I will forbear, I will spare you. If I had a congregation of men, I would not spare them one whit.

The Bishop is to be the husband of one wife. And as for old Paul, everybody says he lived and died a bachelor; but he said all things were lawful for him, and that he had power to lead about a sister, a wife, as well as other Apostles, and as the brethren of the Lord, and Cephas. Paul did not make known all things, for all things were not lawful to tell. He said himself, he knew a man that was caught up to the third heavens, and heard things unlawful to utter. If he did not take a wife, and multiply, and replenish the earth, he did not fulfil the first great fundamental law of nature.

There are many living now who are bachelors. I do not complain of the very old men, for they cannot help themselves at all times, but I am going to complain of the old bachelors; and I tell you what it is, if you do not step forward and marry, and try to carry on the great work of Jehovah, it will be left for a better man to do than you. [Voice in the stand, "There is but one old bachelor in the Territory, and he has gone to the States."] O! I beg your pardon; President Young says he does not know of but one old bachelor in all the Territory of Utah, and he has gone to the States; therefore I have nothing more to say on this particular point. Look abroad upon the world at large, and how many are there who are too niggardly to take a wife, and support her and her offspring honorably, and rear up a family that will reflect honor upon them in their old age! No--they cannot afford to do this, but they go where they can gratify their fleshly desires, leaving the consequences altogether with the confiding females whom they dishonor, and who in that state despair of ever being reinstated in society with a good character, give themselves to prostitution, and in rottenness go down to a premature grave with ten thousand curses on the heads of their deceivers.

Do you suppose these things are going to escape the all-seeing eye of the Great Jehovah? And will He not visit the guilty sensualist with a dreadful punishment? He will. Why not in honorable wedlock raise up offspring to glorify God? Why this niggardly disposition? No wonder the Lord Almighty sends the pestilence to lay them waste, and reduce nations and cities to ruins.

Brethren and sisters, it is for us to have the light of truth shining in our eyes, and honor that truth in all our intercourse with one another.

The Bishop shall have but one wife. If you were in a country where only one wife is allowed by law, then you would be obliged to have but one. What shall I say? A Bishop in England, where he knew polygamy to be contrary to law, must have but one wife; if you want another, and the law will not allow it, you must go where it is allowed by law. It was the case with the Bishops in olden times. We must submit to the laws of man until he shall reign whose right it is to reign.

This is the cord that shall revolutionize the whole world, and it will make the United States tremble from the very head to the foot; it is like leaven hid in three measures of meal until the whole is leavened. There is such a tide of irresistible arguments that, like the grand Mississippi, it bears on its bold current everything that dares to oppose its course.

Says one, "Why is it that men in your society may have more than one wife? What is the policy of it?" The men of God who hold the Priesthood of heaven, and imbibe the light of the Holy Ghost, have the privilege and right. Now let me illustrate one thing, and let me bring it home to you. There may be some under the sound of my voice that the case will fit. Some man will perhaps marry a wife of his youth. She dies--he loved her as he loves himself; and her memory ever lingers about his heart. He marries another, and she dies, and he loved her equally as well. He marries a third, and so on, and he loved them all. By and bye he dies, and he dies with devoted affection and love to them all.

Now in the resurrection, which of these wives will he claim? There is no difference in his love to any of them, and they have all perhaps borne children to him. He loves the children of one mother as well as the children of another. What say you? Which shall he have in the resurrection? Why, let him have the whole of them. To whom are they nearer allied?

There is a case opposite to this, where a woman married a husband, and he died, and so on, until she was married to seven husbands, and then she died. The question was asked the Savior, "Whose wife will she be in the resurrection!" for they all had her. The Savior gave a curious answer. Says he, "In the resurrection they neither marry, nor are given in marriage, but are as the angels of God." Now tell me how the angels are in heaven, and then we shall have the secret.

It is said, "In the last days, saith God, I will pour out of my Spirit upon all flesh: and your sons and your daughters shall prophesy, and your young men shall see visions, and your old men shall dream dreams: and on my servants and on my handmaidens I will pour out in those days of my Spirit; and they shall prophecy." You are praying every day, "Thy kingdom come, and thy will be done on earth as it is in heaven." You never can know how it is done in heaven, unless you can see it by vision; or the kingdom, when it does come, unless it is revealed to you by the spirit of prophecy, or in dreams and visions; then you know it.

This is the benefit of dreams and visions, although this power is lightly spoken of, and repudiated in the Christian world. The revelation of the Almighty from God to a man who holds the Priesthood, and is enlightened by the Holy Ghost, whom God designs to make a ruler and a governor in His eternal kingdom is, that he may have many wives, that when he goes yonder to another sphere he may still continue to perpetuate his species, and of the increase of his kingdom and government there shall be no end, says Daniel. How does the kingdom of God increase, but by the increase of its subjects? Everything increases, everything multiplies. As brother Benson said this morning, even the musquitoes [sic] of Nebraska increase and multiply. If they do, why not high orders of the creation have a better right? These musquitoes and insects are the result of a fallen world, but by and bye there will be nothing to hurt or destroy in all God's holy mountain.

These men of God who are married here by the authority of heaven are sealed on earth and in heaven. The good old book says, that which is sealed on earth is sealed in heaven; and whosesoever sins ye remit on earth shall be remitted in heaven, and whatsoever ye bind on earth shall be bound in heaven. That Priesthood that has not this power is no better than a rope of sand. The true Priesthood alone possesses it. The Priesthood that has not this power is a mock Priesthood, and not the Priesthood of the Almighty. Little did the world know when they treated the Savior as they did, that he held their destiny in his hands; the world knew him not; he came to his own and they received him not; but the time will come that they will know him, and the power of his Priesthood.

When the servants of God and their wives go to heaven there is an eternal union, and they will multiply and replenish the world to which they are going.

It is not every man in the United States that can be the president, or that can be a governor, or a judge, but all are within the pale of the government of the United States, though they do not all bear rule; many are called, and few are chosen. But in yonder world those who bear the Priesthood, and by their faith and obedience obtain the sanction of the Almighty, they are sealed on earth and in heaven, and will be exalted to rule and govern for ever; while those who would not listen to the holy commandments, and died without having a wife sealed to them, are angels; they are lower spirits, and servants to them that rule. Therefore, this family of old, which the Savior spoke of, saying, "In the resurrection they neither marry, nor are given in marriage," are not Gods, but angels, who neither marry nor are given in marriage, while the men that magnify their callings are they that bear rule, and hold dominion, and receive their crown, and are one with the Savior, as he is one with the Father. Hence, he that is faithful over a few things shall be made ruler over many things.

I have a few words more to say, and a great deal more can be said; for I have only just dipped into the subject a little. I want to say a few things more, and perhaps this is the most fitting occasion on which they could be said. You never see a "Mormon" man who bears the Priesthood, unless it is some characters that only bear it in form, who are devoid of principle, who have transgressed, and have escaped being dealt with--I say you never see a true-hearted "Mormon" man running after a lewd woman; but there are women among the Latter-day Saints who are loose in their conduct, notwithstanding they have embraced the Gospel. We only wish to apply this where it belongs; do not any of you have your feelings hurt, for God knows I would hold the virtuous and good as sacred as I would my own life. At the same time I am bound to speak in plainness, and I feel that the Spirit is on me now, I am warmed with it, and it presses me to speak on this subject, and to speak it out. There are families in this town that have bowed externally to the yoke of Christ, but they are as corrupt as hell, and I can point where they are, in what direction they dwell. When I approach their habitations, I feel that they are an abomination in my sight. "Have you any tangible evidence of this?" Yes, I have, and more than I want, which I shall keep to myself, but the day will come when it will all come out. Do you see "Mormon" men running there? No. Wherever you find a house among the Latter-day Saints where no "Mormon" men go, you may know it is not all sound in Denmark. I will tell you whom you see there in particular--men who fear not God nor regard man. What have I got to say concerning women that will come into the Church and kingdom of God, and bring dishonor upon themselves, and endeavour to bring it upon the whole Church, by cohabiting with those cursed scapegraces who are passing through here to California who make their boast of of [sic] what they did in Great Salt Lake City? I know their secret talk in their chambers, for the Spirit of God searcheth all things. It may not be with me to the same extent all the time, but sometimes the whole vision of my mind is lit up, and I see and understand it all.

I am going to say something upon those who dishonor the Church and kingdom of God in this way. I will tell you what shall happen to those men and women who commit lewdness, and go and boast of it, and laugh in the face of heaven. The day shall come when their flesh shall rot upon their bones, and as they are walking it shall drop, and become a nauseous stink upon the highway. Now go and boast that you can get all you want for a dress pattern, or a yard of ribbon; go and boast of it, and the Lord Almighty shall curse you all the day long. [Voice in the stand, "Amen."] And when you step, chunks of your flesh shall drop off your bones, and stink enough to sicken a dog.

I speak this to both men and women that practise this iniquity in the midst of this people; and if you do not refrain from such intercourse, this prediction shall begin to take effect, and by this you shall know whether I have spoken in the name of the Lord, or in the name of Orson Hyde. For such abominable practices to come in our midst under the robes of sanctity, because there are liberal, holy, and righteous principles practised by the Saints, I say, curse their habitation and their persons; and if this is your mind, let all Israel say amen. [The whole of the congregation at the top of their voices said, "Amen!"] And let these contemptible wretches feel the "Mormon" spirit, not by "Mormon" hands, but by the power of God on high.

I feel charged with the Holy Ghost sent down from heaven, and it burns in my heart like a flame, and this is the testimony I bear. If I do mingle in the streets with the crowd to engage in business as any other man, I am not always asleep, and insensible to what is passing around me. I do not profess to know a great deal, but some things I do know, and some things I do not know.

I have endeavored to illustrate this subject for the benefit of the honest inquirer, I have only just touched it, endeavoring to throw out a few hints for your consideration, that you may know we are not without some reason for our faith and practice touching the subject of polygamy. I wish you to mind the admonition I have given. I have given it to you in faith; I have given it to you regardless of consequences, for I ask no odds of any body, except of my Father in heaven, and of my brethren whose hearts I know to be pure; and I want to be identified with them in time and in all eternity, and with my sisters too; and wish to be exalted with them, and them with me, where the Saints may join hands after passing through much tribulation, and gaining crowns, to rejoice together for ever and ever.

I feel as though I had borne a faithful testimony, and I now say, in the presence of God and angels, that I have given the guilty persons warning, and my garments are clean from your blood. Take warning, and never do a thing that will throw dishonor upon the Saints of the Most High.

May God add His blessing, and preserve us to His heavenly kingdom, which may He grant. Amen.

JD 2:75-88

OBEDIENCE PRODUCES CONFIDENCE--CONSECRATION--CONCENTRATION OF INTERESTS--ETC.

Discourse, by President Heber C. Kimball, Delivered in the Tabernacle, Great Salt Lake City, March 1, 1857.

A more sensitive man than brother Joseph Smith never lived, and that sensitiveness was in proportion to the light he had. So it is with brother Brigham, and so it is with brother Heber, and so it is with brother Daniel, and it will increase upon him as he presses his way forward, and works in the harness, and becomes used to it; and he will be just as good a teamhorse as the Lord ever used, and I know it.

I will speak of brother Joseph Young. I often speak of him; he is one of the most sensitive men that ever walked on the earth, and that is in proportion to the light he has, and if the Lord had not laid His hands on him and said, "My servant Joseph, be thou sick and go to thy bed and rest, he would have been in his grave long ago. His late sickness saved his life. That may be a curiosity to you, but the best days I ever had with regard to the happiness of my spirit, have been when I was prostrate on my bed, and in reality could not help myself. People will say, "O how I pity such and such brethren and sisters, because they are unwell." If persons would appreciate their blessings when they are on beds of sickness, and say, "Father, thy will be done, and not mine," there would be no room for that pity. When necessary in God's providences towards me, I would as soon lay on a bed of sickness as to do anything else, for we have got to learn that lesson. I have to struggle, and brother Brigham has to struggle to exist here on the earth.

I will say, not that I speak of these things to boast, that if this people, both men and women, would pray, and that devoutly before God in their secret places, one quarter as much as brother Brigham, and I, and brother Joseph Young do, you would see different days from what you see to-day. When Jesus came to his people on this continent, and appeared in their midst, they could not at first realize and appreciate him. They saw him and felt the wounds in his side, in his hands, and in his feet, and he talked with them and instructed them, and chose and instructed twelve disciples. And after healing their sick and blessing their children, he administered bread and wine to the people, and taught them to "watch and pray always." He could not heal their sick, until through prayer they had become humble, and got the power of God on them. And when he had done this he said, bring all your children, and he blessed them one by one, and the power of God rested on them, and angels descended from heaven and encircled them round about, and ministered to them before the eyes of the people.

What do you suppose we are going to do with you? Are you ever going to be prepared to see God, Jesus Christ, His angels, or comprehend His servants, unless you take a faithful and prayerful course? Did you actually know Joseph Smith? No. Do you know brother Brigham? No. Do you know brother Heber? No, you do not. Do you know the Twelve? You do not, if you did, you would begin to know God, and learn that those men who are chosen to direct and counsel you are near kindred to God and to Jesus Christ, for the keys, power, and authority of the kingdom of God are in that lineage. I speak of these things with a view to arouse your feelings and your faithfulness towards God the Father, and His Son Jesus Christ, that you may pray and be humble, and penitent.

When Jesus Christ came to this earth, he came to fulfil the law, and he taught the people to seek to the Father with a broken heart and contrite spirit, and then whatever they asked He would give. If you so come unto Him, repenting and being sorry for your sins, then He will hear you and forgive you, and He will forgive this whole people. Why? Because brother Brigham never would have said to you that God would forgive you if you would repent, unless he had received some intimation of that kind from the Father and the Son, and the Holy Ghost. But brother Brigham told you the truth, and the Lord will forgive you, if you stop sinning now, and begin anew to-day to work righteousness with full purpose of heart. Then through continued faithfulness that Spirit, light, and glory will rest upon you, that brother Joseph has been talking about this morning.

I am speaking of these things to comfort you, for they comfort me. I am talking to you of nothing more than what I know, feel, and have experienced. What brother Joseph Young has said, is good. I feel very well in my body and in my spirit, that is, I feel well in regard to the things of God. I feel well, because there are some trying to live their religion, and worship their God in spirit and in truth. When they hear the servants of God declare the truth here, they understand it, and the seed springs up, and brings forth fruit to the glory of God, and that fruit will remain. But there are others who hear the word and do not conceive; they sit and hear the voice of God speaking through His servants, and like the sound thereof, but the moment they leave this place they forget it.

Some say that they have not faith, that they cannot believe. What is faith? It is confidence. What is confidence? It is faith. Some people are striving and striving to get faith, when saving faith is simply confidence in God, flowing from walking in obedience to His commandments. When you have confidence in yourself, in any man, woman, or child, you have faith; and when you have not confidence, you have not faith. I believe they are co-partners, and the principle of faith and confidence is synonymous to me.

If you have not faith to deed your property over to the Trustee in Trust, it is because you have not confidence in the Trustee in Trust. If you had confidence in him, you would have faith in him. You may pay your tithing--you may tithe your sage, mint, and catnip, and this and that, and the other, and after all you may be leaving the more weighty matters undone. It is not best to become stereotyped in paying tithing and stop at that; but if you are going to become stereotyped, I wish you to stereotype the whole edition, and let it remain so, and then go on and make another. I do not object to your stereotyping one letter at a time, if you will go on through the whole edition.

In regard to deeding over your property, no one compels you to do it. I do not compel you to do it, the Trustee in Trust does not, God does not; but He says that if you will do this, that and the other thing which He has counselled for our good, do so, and prove Him. He goes to work and proves us, as we go to work and prove one another under various circumstances. The Lord says, cast in your tithes, and then your offerings. Tithing is one thing, and offerings are another. And when that is done, consecrate your property to the Church, and make strong the hands of our President, and he will handle and distribute it to the best advantage. We are to be tried in all things, like unto Abraham, and God even told Abraham to offer up his son Isaac. He went and built the altar, got the wood and the knife, and was ready to do the work; but instead of offering up his son, the Lord said to him, take this ram and offer him up, and put your son to usury, and he shall become a multitude of nations--his offspring shall be as numerous as the sands on the sea shore, and as the stars in the firmament. It will be just so with the property deeded over to the Trustee in Trust; every man becomes a steward, and puts out his property to usury. The principle of the consecration is to hold property secure and in the channel of blessings and increase.

Our property should not be dearer to us than salvation, and should freely be put to the best use for building up the kingdom of God. To illustrate my ideas, I will use a comparison. Here is my little finger, does not the blood go into that finger as freely and as fully, in proportion as it goes into my leg, or into my arm? Does it always stay there? Does that little finger become selfish--superstitious with the principle of idolatry--and never restore that blood to the fountain? No, for if it did, the fountain would be weakened, and the finger would wither, because of an interrupted communication. How can this Church exist upon any other principle than that of free interchange according to the dictation of the head? My finger restores back the blood to the fountain, where it again becomes impregnated with the principles of life, and then when it goes back again is not that finger impregnated with the power of my vitality--of my attributes? If that is a fact, when we take the same course with the things of God and turn in our property, it will become empowered with the attributes of God and His Son Jesus Christ and the Holy Ghost, and of all those who act with them in the eternal worlds, and from them to us, and from us back to the throne of God. And except we become impregnated with saving principles as they exist with God, with Jesus Christ, with angels, with Peter and with Joseph, you may bid farewell to salvation, every soul of you.

I wish that this whole people would so get religion that brother Brigham and myself, and other good men could always freely and fully teach you all things pertaining to salvation, and show you your condition, even as the Lord views it. Here is the kingdom of God, here are the Prophet and the Apostles, the Patriarch, and all the leading men of Israel, and where is there a man in Europe, or in any other country, who sprung from this Church, but what sprung from the authority, the life, vitals, and power of this Church and kingdom? If he has not got his power unto salvation in this Church, he has not any power towards an exaltation in the celestial kingdom of our God. And those who have power from the true source have not predominance over those who hold the keys in advance of them, for the kingdom of God is a kingdom of order. How can you become impregnated with the spirit and power of God, except you become impregnated through us? There is no true path, except to do as you are told by those whom the Lord has called and chosen, and placed to direct you.

I do not care so much whether you have faith or not, for if you have confidence in yourselves, I would risk the confidence you should have in us. And if you have lost confidence in yourselves, you will not have much confidence in your brethren; and in that case I want to know what confidence you can have in your God? The Lord often takes a course to try the confidence of His people, for He planted a branch of the olive tree in the poorest spot in all the land of His vineyard, and He caused it to yield much fruit that was good. That was considered a marvellous work, and one of His servants said, "How camest thou hither to plant this tree, or this branch of the tree? for behold it was the poorest spot in all the land of thy vineyard. And the Lord of the vineyard said unto him, counsel me not, but go to and do all things as I command you."

Now suppose I should say, here, John, William, and Richard, I want you to go up near the arsenal and dig a well, and when you have dug ten feet you will find water. They would be very apt to say, "We have not a particle of confidence in that operation." I would reply, I do not care about that; it is the well I want, and that will afford water. They go to work without one particle of confidence in what I say, and dig to the depth of ten feet, and come to good water. By so doing, have they not obtained knowledge without confidence? Yes, by their works. And Jesus says, by your works shall you be judged, and by your works shall you be justified. John, Bill, and Dick, dig the well, and I have accomplished my design with them, though they had not a particle of confidence in me, nor in God. And when they have found water, they say, "That gives me confidence in you, brother Heber, and in your God." The result of their works gives them confidence. It may stimulate some of you to go to work upon that principle, viz., to do as you are told, without knowing whether you will get water or not.

Well, go to work and dig the Big Cottonwood canal on the same principle. Begin to-morrow morning, and do not cease until that canal is done, and I will warrant the water to come, and when it comes, that will increase your confidence. Brethren, will you all with your Bishops lay aside everything that is not of greater importance, and go to work on that canal until it is finished? If you will work, instead of merely saying you will, and go to with all your hearts, it will be but a short time before you see the rock being boated on it for our Temple; and it need not be only a few years before the Temple is built, wherein you will receive your endowments and blessings. And God our Father will protect us and give us good peace, until we have accomplished that work and many other things. He will strengthen our feet and fill our granaries.

Will you go to work at once on the canal, letting your Bishops lead out and you follow? If you will, raise your right hands. [All hands were raised.] If you live up to the covenant now made, you will soon accomplish the work; and it will be but a few days before the ground will be in readiness for ploughing and seeding, and God will bless the earth and strengthen it to yield an abundance, through your going and doing that little work, and letting the water into that canal, so that we can boat rock from the quarry unto this place. Let us go to and do, instead of merely saying. That is drawing our feelings into the one reservoir.

Upon the same principle, let every man render over his property with an eternal deed that cannot be broken; throw it all into the big reservoir. Suppose that one puts in one drop, another two, another ten, and another a hundred, do you not see, when you throw in your property--your substance--into one reservoir, that it makes us all one, and that you cannot become one without this principle? You may work to all eternity, and never connect the branch with the vine, upon any other principle than that of putting your property and temporal blessings with your spiritual interests, whereby they will both become one. If you do not do that, I do not mean in one thing only, but in everything that God requires of you by His servants, if you do not bring your substance forward and lay it down at the Apostles' feet, you will be stripped. Brother Brigham is the chief Apostle of Jesus, and he is our President, our Prophet, and our leader, and we the Twelve are his brethren, and you have got to lay down your substance at their feet, as the Saints did in the days of the ancient Apostles of Jesus.

Look at Ananias and Sapphira. I have heard you read their history a great many times, and talk about it. They came with a part of their substance, and lied about it. You may do as you have a mind to. In one sense, we do not care whether you lie, or tell the truth. If you tell the truth and do right, who is blessed? Is it any one but yourselves? It is not brother Brigham, nor brother Heber, only in connection with you, inasmuch as you take a course to do right; for being members of the same body to which we are connected, it influences the whole body, and the whole body is blessed at the same time. It does not particularly make any difference with us, as individuals.

You have got to render an account of everything you have, for we are all stewards. You Bishops, Seventies, High Priests, Elders, Priests, Teachers, Deacons, and members, where did you get the Priesthood and authority you hold? It came from this very authority, the First Presidency that sits here in this stand. There was an authority before us, and we got our authority from that, and you got it from us, and this authority is with the First Prisidency [sic]. Now do not go off and say that you are independent of that authority. Where did you get your wives? Who gave them to you? By what authority were they given to you? Where did you get anything?'

If you do not take the course you have been told to take, and as I am trying to tell you, viz., to render all you have on this earth, every man in this Church and kingdom will be as bare when he leaves this earth as he will find himself when he gets out of it for he cannot even take his shroud with him nor a pair of stockings. I do not care if he has forty wives and a thousand children, every soul of them will be taken from him. Your wives are given to you as a stewardship to improve upon in building up and establishing the kingdom of God, and your children are given to you as a stewardship. Where did their spirits come from? Did they come from you? No; they came from God. Who is the Father of those spirits? God, and He will require them of you, and those spirits have also got to give an account to their Father from whom they came; they have got to render up an account. Thus you see, that you have to render an account of your wives and children, of your substance, and everything that pertains to this earth, and you cannot avoid it, without suffering a loss.

I want to get you to live your religion, and worship our God. I am not troubled about our not prospering; I trouble myself about living my religion and being faithful to the things of God, and that leads me to confidence, if not in myself, in my leader. It is not so much matter [sic--phrase] about my trying to obtain confidence in myself, or in you. We are to be connected like a vine, and then when we receive any good thing we will become impregnated with God, with Jesus Christ, with the Holy Ghost, and with angels, and it is the only way in which we can become one.

I feel as brother Joseph Young feels. God bless him, and may he live a hundred years, if he wants to. I pray that God may renew him in body and blood, and bless him with every good thing that he desires; also brother Brigham, and brother Daniel, and brother Heber, and every other good man. That is my prayer and my feeling. And may the Lord bless every good woman with the same blessings.

Brethren, tumble in your interest into this great reservoir, and we will drink up the earth. And if you do not do it, as the Lord lives, the First Presidency of this Church and the Twelve will drink you up. If you trifle with me, when I tell you the truth, you will trifle with brother Brigham; and if you trifle with him, you will also trifle with angels and with God, and thus you will trifle yourselves down to hell. You cannot with impunity trifle with God, for the day is too far advanced for that. Do not trouble yourselves about your sins if you have repented of them; and if you have not, it is time you did.

I will say to the Bishops in general, take those who are humble, those who have repented and made restitution, and baptize them for the remission of their sins, and then lay hands upon them, that they may receive the Holy Ghost, and they will receive it, if you take counsel and do right. And you will feel as you never felt before since you were born, and the works of God will continue, if you will do right, for the time has come.

God bless you, peace be with you for ever. Amen.

JD 4:247-253

MAN THE HEAD OF WOMAN--KINGDOM OF GOD--THE SEED OF CHRIST--POLYGAMY--SOCIETY IN UTAH.

A Sermon, by President Orson Hyde, Delivered in Great Salt Lake City.

Dear brethren and sisters, it is with feelings not a little peculiar that I arise to address you on this occasion. By this effort I have solely for my object your edification in the wide field of truth, which has been opened by the "key of knowledge" to our mind's eye, and we are bade to enter and regale ourselves among the undying beauties that flourish spontaneously in this heavenly soil. We wish to be made wiser by a knowledge of true principles, and better by adopting them in all the practical walks of life.

Had I copied the style of address adopted by the fashionable world, I might have said, "Ladies and gentlemen," placing the fair in the van, but as this would only be to reverse the order of our being through life's thorny way, ordained and established by heaven's law, I have felt, and still feel, to observe the spirit of that law and that order, not only in my manner of address, but in all the varied duties, responsibilities, and pleasures of life. The hypocritical respect lavished upon females by the etiquette of the world in pushing them forward, and in exciting their vanity by making them most conspicuous in all the novels and romances which, like so much trash, have flooded society and cursed the land, is only to make them a more easy prey to the unbridled sensuality and the ungodly lusts of their benighted authors. Flattery is food for the silly and shallow brained, but a wise heart and pure hand will never administer it.

The order of heaven places man in the front rank; hence he is first to be addressed. Woman follows under the protection of his counsels, and the superior strength of his arm. Her desire should be unto her husband, and he should rule over her. I will here venture the assertion, that no man can be exalted to a celestial glory in the kingdom of God whose wife rules over him; and as the man is not without the woman, nor the woman without the man in the Lord, it follows a matter of course, that the woman who rules over her husband, thereby deprives herself of a celestial glory.

[Here the speaker was interrupted by the question from the congregation, "What, then, will become of Prince Albert and Queen Victoria?" The speaker replied, General and eternal principles are too stubborn to yield to individual accommodation. They must see to their own affairs.]

But to my subject: The day in which we live is an important one--important to the world at large, and to us as a people. As time is measured off to us by the day, by the week, and by the year, our quantum will soon be run off, and we be summoned to render an account of the use and improvement we have made of it. Let the question now arise in every breast, Am I acting well my part while I occupy the stage of life? Remember that your daily prayer to God is, "Thy kingdom come, and Thy will be done on earth, as it is done in heaven." Remember, also, that we are the favoured and chosen people to whom that kingdom is come, and it will continue with us, provided our energies, coupled with the wisdom and power of God, be directed to that object--an object for which all Christendom is praying to be accomplished; and one, too, against which their skill, learning, and power will be arrayed. Even the devils in hell will burst forth from their fiery cells to unite with the fallen sons of earth, to oppose the kingdoms of this world becoming the kingdom of our God. The kings and rulers of the earth will not willingly cast their crowns and sceptres at the feet of the Priesthood, and worship the God of Hosts. His almighty power, in judgments, alone will humble them into this submission. "He shall send forth judgment unto victory." Let strict integrity and purity of heart and life be our bulwarks, and the faith of Abraham, Moses, Daniel, Shadrach, Meshach, and Abednego, be our shield and fortress of strength now, and in the day of temptation and trial. To incite you to diligence and perseverance, let me tell you that our foes are not only strong, but wily; and yet to encourage you--to inspire you with faith and hope, allow me to say that God is stronger and more wily than they. The Almighty never did, neither will He ever display His power in behalf of His people until they are brought into tried and straightened places; and what if some of us should lay down our lives for Christ's sake? We all have to die at some time; and if we are but in the faithful discharge of our duty, it should matter not to us when or by what means we go. Our enemies may say, for righteousness sake we kill thee not, but for thine own wickedness and perverseness.

What persecutors of the followers of Jesus ever acknowledged that they martyred or killed the Saints for righteousness sake? None! They claimed that they did it on account of their wickedness; and if they never have made this acknowledgement, do you think they ever will? No! With a blind and maddened zeal against the Saints, strengthened by the eternal hatred and jealousy of the fallen angels, will they fill the cup of their iniquity and ripen in the glare of their oppression for the judgments of Almighty God.

Are we everywhere spoken against? Is almost every newspaper and journal, with a thousand and one anonymous letter writers, pouring forth their spleen, animadversions, and maledictions upon the Saints in Utah? Do they wish and intend to blow up a storm--a tempest to burst upon our heads with all the fury of the combined elements to sweep us from the face of the earth? Or secretely [sic] and under cover, do they intend to rig a purchase to prey upon the peace and happiness of the Saints who have fled from the face of the "serpent," unprotected and unredressed, to this desolate land, to which no other people would come until after we came and killed the snakes, built the bridges, proved the country, raised bread and built houses for them to come to, a land where no other people can or will dwell, should the Mormous [sic] leave it!

Why this hatred and ill-will against you? What have you done to provoke it? We have rebuked iniquity; and, in some instances, in rather high places. But the real cause is explained by our Saviour: "Ye are not of the world, but I have chosen you out of the world, therefore the world hate you."

Remember that God not only rules the storm, but visits the secret chambers. He can hush the storm, and say to the winds, "Peace, be still," and catch the fowler in his own snare.

The professed purity of this generation will not allow the institutions of Utah to exist undisturbed, if they can devise any scheme to disturb them. It is true that the people of Utah believe in and practise polygamy. Not because our natural desires lead us into that condition and state of life, but because our God hath commanded it, and wishing to comply with that as well as with all others of His commands, we are as we are. We also wish to be counted Abraham's children, to whom the promises were made, and also with whom the covenants were established; and being told that if we are the children of Abraham, we will do the works of Abraham, we are not a little anxious to do as he did. Among other things that he did, he took more than one wife. In this he was not alone, for this example was copied by most of the ancient worthies and others who succeeded him under the same everlasting covenant. Even the wisest and best men--men after God's own heart, entered the most deeply into this practice. Nor was this practice limited to the days of the Old Testament.

It will be borne in mind that once on a time, there was a marriage in Cana of Galilee; and on a careful reading of that transaction, it will be discovered that no less a person than Jesus Christ was married on that occasion. If he was never married, his intimacy with Mary and Martha, and the other Mary also whom Jesus loved, must have been highly unbecoming and improper to say the best of it.

I will venture to say that if Jesus Christ were now to pass through the most pious countries in Christendom with a train of women,. such as used to follow him, fondling about him, combing his hair, anointing him with precious ointment, washing his feet with tears, and wiping them with the hair of their heads and unmarried, or even married, he would be mobbed, tarred, and feathered, and rode, not on an ass, but on a rail. What did the old Prophet mean when he said (speaking of Christ), "He shall see his seed, prolong his days, &c." Did Jesus consider it necessary to fulfil every righteous command or requirement of his Father?

He most certainly did. This he witnessed by submitting to baptism under the hands of John. "Thus it becometh us to fulfil all righteousness," said he. Was it God's commandment to man, in the beginning, to multiply and replenish the earth? None can deny this, neither that it was a righteous command; for upon an obedience to this, depended the perpetuity of our race. Did Christ come to destroy the law or the Prophets, or to fulfil them? He came to fulfil. Did he multiply, and did he see his seed? Did he honour his Father's law by complying with it, or did he not? Others may do as they like, but I will not charge our Saviour with neglect or transgression in this or any other duty.

At this doctrine the long-faced hypocrite and the sanctimonious bigot will probably cry, blasphemy! Horrid perversion of God's word! Wicked wretch! He is not fit to live! &c., &c. But the wise and reflecting will consider, read, and pray. If God be not our Father, grandfather, or great grandfather, or some kind of a father in reality, in deed and in truth, why are we taught to say, "Our Father who art in heaven?" How much soever [sic] of holy horror of this doctrine may excite in persons not impregnated with the blood of Christ, and whose minds are consequently dark and benighted, it may excite still more when they are told that if none of the natural blood of Christ flows in their veins, they are not the chosen or elect of God. Object not, therefore, too strongly against the marriage of Christ, but remember that in the last days, secret and hidden things must come to light, and that your life also (which is the blood) is hid with Christ in God.

Abraham was chosen of God for the purpose of raising up a chosen seed, and a peculiar people unto His name. Jesus Christ was sent into the world for a similar purpose, but upon a more extended scale. Christ was the seed of Abraham, so reckoned. To these, great promises were made; one of which was, that in Abraham and in his seed, which was Christ, all the families of the earth should be blessed. When? When the ungodly or those not of their seed should be cut off from the earth, and no family remaining on earth except their own seed. Then in Abraham and in Christ, all the families and kindreds of the earth will be blessed-- Satan bound, and the millenium [sic] fully come. Then the meek will inherit the earth, and God's elect reign undisturbed, at least, for one thousand years.

Is there no way provided for those to come into this covenant relation who may not possess, in their veins, any of the blood of Abraham or of Christ? Yes! By doing the works of Abraham and of Christ in the faith of Abraham and of Christ; not in unbelief and unrighteousness, like the wicked world who have damned themselves in their own corruption and unbelief. If thou wilt believe on the Lord Jesus Christ, and repent of thy sins, and put them all away, and forsake them for ever, and turn unto the Lord our God, and serve Him with all thy might, mind, and strength, the Holy Ghost will change the vile body, quicken and renew thy spirit and natural system, so that thou shalt lay off or overcome that fallen nature which is in the body with its sins, and be created anew in Christ Jesus, with a new heart and a new spirit, even the Holy Ghost; this will cause your spirits to cry, Abba, Father. Your lips may even now cry, "Abba, Father;" but your spirit cannot until it is renovated; and lip service, you know, is mockery before God. We are to worship God in spirit and in truth, and with the understanding also. But if you wish to destroy us for doing the works of Abraham and of Christ, know ye that God will curse you; and neither He nor His people will allow you to have any part in the covenant of promise; and neither in Abraham, nor yet in Christ can ye be blessed. There is something more implied in this change often alluded to by all professing Christians than is usually considered. It is, nevertheless, scripturally and philosophically true.

During the late session of the Legislature, a very polite note was received by that body from Mr. Van Emman, agent of the American Bible Society, who wished to have the members call at his depository and examine his Bibles, quality, and prices, and to advertise them in the various localities to which they were about to repair, and also to lay before them the object of the society in sending the Bibles to Utah. The Legislature thought proper to appoint a committee to wait upon Mr. V., examine his books, &c., and being a member of the House, I, with brother F. D. Richards, was appointed said committee. In the discharge of our duties, I remarked to Mr. Van Emman, who, by the by, received us very gentlemanly, that the society which he had the honour to represent, no doubt considered us degraded and almost beyond the reach of Bible truth. He replied, that they did not consider us so degraded as we might think they did; but that it was the design of the society to put the word of God into the hands of every man in the world, Utah not excepted. I replied, that this was very good. But however charitable and benevolent the designs of that society may be, so far as Utah is concerned, they have sent us the wrong book if they wish to reclaim us from the belief in and practice of Polygamy: for instead of its reclaiming us, it confirms us in our belief and practice, and no where condemns it; and, hence, we are conscientious in our manner of life, having the word of God which you bring us for our standard. Although our faith and practice are such as we declare unto you, yet no people on earth look with greater abhorence [sic] and indignation upon a violation of the principles that govern us than we do. No man or woman among us, not of our faith, that behaves himself, and violates not our laws and regulations, has any occasion to fear molestation. But if he or she violates them and will not desist, I cannot vouch for his safety, member of our Church or not, neither can I insure his house to stand.

We have had, and still have among us, men who write back to the States glaring accounts of our character and conduct, and bitter complants [sic] of our treatment toward them; but it would be hard for them to detail the awful treatment they pretend to represent. We do not often act without a cause; and one, too, which, with them, we are willing to meet at the bar of God and answer to our treatment. We have been unmercifully forced to come to Utah; but we force no one else to come; yet if they do come, we want them to behave themselves, and attend to their own business. We do not consider an officer of the government to have any more right to commit wickedness than any one else; and if he does, he merits as severe a rebuke, and even more so, for he not only destroys his influence and power to do good, but brings dishonour upon the power that sent him. I would say to our friends, that I have no hesitancy in recommending the Bibles of Mr. Van Emman. They are, most un- [sic] unquestionably, a well got up book, and afforded much cheaper than they can usually be bought in this place. You who want the Bible, I would advise to avail yourselves of this favourable opportunity.

Are the "Mormons" an industrious people? Every body says they are, I say we are, and for the rest, our works may speak. One circumstance, however, I will mention. Some letter writer, probably of the *corps militaire*, thought it deeply degrading that the wife of Orson Hyde, chief of the Apostles, should take in washing for a living: but if she had kept some house other than a laundry, not necessary to say what kind, it might have elevated her in the gentleman's estimation, to the ranks of fashionable life.

If this gentleman had ever ascended the Nile, he would have learned that the native men who tow and propel boats up that stream in which travelers are conveyed, are mostly in a state of perfect nudity. This they do on account of the exceeding warm weather, and also for convenience sake, being as often in the water as out of it. They do not wish to be encumbered with clothing. European gentlemen, travelling with their families up the Nile, often purchase them entire suits, not out of any particular regard they have for the natives, but out of special regard for the modesty and delicacy of their families. So also some of our good and industrious wives, who are not above doing whatever is necessary to be done in their sphere, often condescend (however humiliating the service) to wash up a stranger's linen, that he may appear in "Mormon society" without being particularly obnoxious. Industry is our element.

Is persevering industry a faithful index to all the crime, debauchery, and wickedness with which we are charged? Men of reputation and sense, consider! Can such a mass of corrupt beings as we are represented, hang together, be united and submit to rigid rule and discipline so long--encounter every hardship and privation that we have, and still be cheerful and buoyant with hope? There may be some little family irregularities occasionally, but they are soon adjusted. Are there no family disturbances among other people? I have often read of the husband murdering the wife, and the wife the husband, among those who consider it a high crime to have more than one wife. This is a thing of frequent occurrence. But who ever knew of a "Mormon" intentionally killing any of his wives, or any wife her husband? No one! I answer again, no one!

All things, now, candidly and impartially considered, to what conclusion must the uprejudiced [sic] and candid arrive respecting the "Mormons?" It seems to me that they must conclude something as follows:

There may be those among them, both male and female, who do not behave as they ought, for their net catches of every kind, both good and bad. The crucible or refining pot is Utah. There the heat is raised to a degree that causes the pure to melt and sink beneath, out of sight of the casual observer, while the dross, slag, or scoria meets every eye, and forms the principal subjects for our letter writers and numerous Editors to display their talents upon, while the pure metal is consolidated beneath, unobserved and unnoticed; and yet this dross is a faithful index to the actual existence of pure metal near by. May not this generation have bright and keen eyes, and still not able to see; ears, but not able to hear; and hearts, yet not able to understand? After all that has been said, done, and written about the "Mormons," Mormon religion, &c., may there not be a principle incorporated with them that flows in a deep channel which operates upon their hearts and consciences, and that principle emanate from God Himself? Are there not tangible facts connected with their religion and history sufficient to warrant this conclusion? Ye juries of nations consider well--weigh the subject impartially--remember that life and death are involved in the issue! Should there be an existing doubt in your minds, you are bound to give the accused the benefit of that doubt; and though it may not accord with popular practice for an attorney to be a witness in behalf of his client, yet knowing his innocence and the justice of his cause--the rectitude of his intention, the purity of his purpose and the general benevolence aimed at as the crowning climax of his exertions and hopes, I cannot refrain from adding my testimony in his behalf.

In the most pious and well-regulated families on earth, there are sometimes occurrences take place of which no member of that family would be proud to speak openly; and which none but a foolish and silly member would speak. On application of this simile to the Church, I am silent. But the bone and sinew of "Mormonism," "Mormon" religion, faith, doctrine, and practice are true as God is true. Joseph Smith and Brigham Young, with as many wives as David and Solomon, (leaving out the concubines) are men after God's own heart; inspired from on high to bring forth the last dispensation of mercy to man--to remove the vail of the covering cast over all people, and light up a flame that will eventually consume the ungodly, and fill the earth with the knowledge and glory of our God; and the "serpent" cannot cast forth waters enough to put it out.

Gentlemen of the jury, you may shudder for me on account of the testimony which I bear, thinking that I shall have it to meet at the court of appeals. I am glad that you are thus sensitive; and allow me to remind you, that you also will have it to meet at the same tribunal! Therefore consider it well; weigh the testimony and arguments in favour of Zion's cause, in a just and even balance, and a true verdict hangs your own destiny for weal or for woe. With these remarks I submit the case.

JD 4:257-264

President Brigham Young,
Feb. 10th, 1867
Portion

Will the time ever come that we can commence and organise this people as a family? It will. Do we know how? Yes; what was lacking in these revelations from Joseph to enable us to do so was revealed to me. Do you think we will ever be one? When we get home to our Father and God will we not wish to be in the family? Will it not be our highest ambition and desire to be reckoned as the sons of the living God, as the daughters of the Almighty, with a right to the household, and the faith that belongs to the household, heirs of the Father, His goods, His wealth, His power, His excellency, His knowledge and wisdom? Ought it not to be our highest ambition to attain to this? How many families do you think there will be then? It is true that we read in the Bible with regard to the twelve tribes of Israel, that they will be gathered together tribe by tribe, and that when they are so gathered they will hear the sentence of the Ancient of Days.

They were commanded never to go out of their own family--the family of Abraham--to seek a partner for life. Did they keep that command? No; but they ran here and there, to the rebellious nations around, and got their wives; and so they continued transgressing and rebelling until the days of Moses, when the gospel was offered to, and utterly rejected by them, and so the Lord gave them the law of Carnal Commandments, in which they were forbidden to marry, as you can read in the Bible. That was a yoke of bondage. And the whole religious world swallow this down as the revelations of the Lord Almighty to His people; they were to His people, but were given in consequence of their rebellion. A great many arguments might be adduced in favor of this, many more, I think, than could be advanced against it. Still we do not care anything about that; we look at facts just as they are. Abraham married his half sister according to the Bible; but there is a discrepancy in the record, for it is stated in his own writings that she was the daughter of his older brother, and he was the chosen of the Lord; and all can read for themselves and see whom Isaac and Jacob got for wives. Did not Jacob, when going to his uncle's house, see Rachel at the well drawing water? Said he, "She is a pretty nice looking girl, I guess I'll help her," and going to do so, he found she was the daughter of the very man to whose house the Lord had sent him; and he liked her well enough to work seven years for her for a wife, and then Leah was palmed on to him, so he worked seven years more for Rachel, and Jacob and his wives were own cousins. Jacob's mother and his wives' father were sister and bother; consequently his wives' grandfather and grandmother--Nehor and Milcah--were his grandfather and grandmother. Besides, Nehor was the brother of Abraham, Jacob's grandfather on his father's side--and Milcah was the sister of Sarah--his grandmother on his father's side. So it was with Israel, in the days of their obedience they were commanded to take partners in their own families; but Israel was finaly divided up into twelve parts, and they will be brought up so. This, however, is something that I understand, and which the people may understand, perhaps, sometime. They will come up tribe by tribe, and the Ancient of Days, He who led Abraham, and talked to Noah, Enoch, Isaac, and Jacob, that very Being will come and judge the twelve tribes of Israel. He will say, "You rebelled, and you have been left to the mercies of the wicked." See the tribe of Judah and the half tribe of Benjamin, that tarried in Palestine when the rest went into the north country, how they have been trampled down!--they have not outgrown it to this day. Take them in England, or across on the Continent, or even in this country, no matter what you do to them, they will not resent it; they submit to it. But they will rise by-and-by and assert their rights and have them. They are the oldest nation in the world, and they have as bright talents as any other people in the world, and the time will come when they will obtain their rights and be restored to the land of their fathers, only be patient about it.

There is another class of individuals to whom I will briefly refer. Shall we call them Christians? They were Christians originally. We cannot be admitted into their social societies, into their places of ghatering at certain times and on certain occasions, beaause [sic] they are afraid of polygamy. I will give you their title that you may all know whom I am talking about it--I refer to the Freemasons. They have refused our brethren membership in their lodge, because they were polygamists. Who was the founder of Freemasonry? They can go back as far as Salomon, and there they stop. There is the king who established this high and holy order. Now was he a polygamist, or was he not? If he did believe in monogamy he did not practise it a great deal, for he had seven hundred wives, and that is more than I have; and he had three hundred concubines, of which I have none that I know of. Yet the whole fraternity throughout Christendom will cry out against this order. "Oh dear, oh dear, oh dear!" What is the matter? "I am in pain," they all cry out, "I am suffering at witnessing the wickedness there is in our land. Here is one of the 'relics of barbarism!'" Yes, one of the relics of Adam, of Enoch, of Noah, of Abraham, of Isaac, of Jacob, of Moses, David, Solomon, the Prophets, of Jesus, and his Apostles. And the other relic they have--you know whether they have used it up or not. Now what does our Bible tell us about this? Under this law of Carnal Commandments, the Lord told Moses to command the people to release their manservants and their maidservants, and forgive their debts once in seven years, and to let their land rest one year in seven; and when seven times seven years had passed over they were commanded to rest seven years, and to release all their manservants and maidservants. How will it be in eternity? We will wait till we get there, for there is no use in telling you; you would not know anything about it. I reckon there will be servants there, and I do not think they will be released once in seven years either; if they are, they will have to be brought right in again, for they will not know how to get their bread, and will have to be taken care of.

A certain portion of the human family have to be looked after and taken care of. If you do not know it, just look through the world and see the very few heads and brains that do all the legislating, and even the obtaining of what the children eat; it is only just a few that do this, out of the inhabitants of the whole earth. We are trying to teach this people to use their brains, that they may obtain knowledge and wisdom to sustain themselves and to dictate for others; that they may be worthy to be made kings and priests to God, which they never can be unless they learn, here or somewhere else, to govern, manage, legislate, and sustain themselves, their families, and friends, even to the making of nations, and nation after nation. If they cannot attain to this, they will have to be servants somewhere.

I say unto you that it is wisdom for us to apply ourselves to the revelations that the Lord has given us, and seek after Him that we may know His will concerning us, that we may be able to abide the day of His wrath, and be counted worthy, through our obedience and faithfulness, to enjoy the blessings that are prepared for the faithful.

We frequently talk about variety. My brother Joseph was talking about the variety in the feelings of this people. Can you see two faces alike in this congregation? If you cannot, you cannot find two spirits alike, you cannot find two who are the same in disposition. And if you search the world over, and all the works of God, you will find that same eternal variety.

We are capable of talking, thinking, and communicating; then we are capable of receiving, and we can receive a little here, and a little there, as the prophet has said, "Line upon line, and precept upon precept," until we come to understanding. This is our privilege; we are capable of doing this, and if we will go to work with our might, and apply ourselves to learning the things of God, you will find there will not be quite so much selfishness as there is now.

I do not know but some people would ask br. Brigham if he is ready to hand over what he has got? just as ready as the man who has only three dimes--just exactly, it is nothing to me. If we could live as one family, and could see that intelligence that is distributed among the minds of the people acted upon, we ahould see no idleness, slothfulness, wastefulness, covetousness, no contention one with another, but every man and woman would be content with what was given them, and with all their souls would seek to obtain salvation, and would not be so eager after a little worldly honor or pleasure, and they would not feel "If I do not have my heaven here, I do not know that I shall ever have it." You cannot have it unless you enjoy the spirit of the Lord, not one of you; you cannot find comfort, solace, or bliss without the Spirit of the Lord. All else contaminates and mars, and is calculated to destroy. As I said to the brethren the other day in the Thirteenth Ward Schoolhouse, with regard to worldly pleasure, comfort, and enjoyment; you may take as much as you please of the Spirit of the Lord, and it will not make your stomach or head ache. You may drink nine cups of strong spiritual drink, and it will not hurt you; but if you drink nine cups of strong tea, see what it will do for you. Let a person that is very thirsty and warm satiate his appetite with cold water, and when he gets through he will perhaps have laid the foundation for death, and may go to an untimely grave, which is frequently done. Excessive eating, drinking, or exercise all tend to the grave; but you may take as much of the Spirit of the Lord as you have a mind to, I do not care if you take a good hearty supper of it and then go right to bed, it will not hurt you in the least; if you take it early in the morning it will not spoil your breakfast. It will never hurt you, but will give life, joy, peace, satisfaction, and contentment; it is light, intelligence, strength, power, glory, wisdom, and finally, it comprehends the kingdoms that are, that were, or that will be, and all that we can contemplate or desire, and will lead us to everlasting life. Only let us have the Spirit of the Lord and we can be happy; while the things of this world, that are so eagerly sought after, all point directly to the grave. Men and women who are trying to make themselves happy in the possession of wealth or power will miss it, for nothing short of the gospel of the Son of God can make the inhabitants of the earth happy, and prepare them to enjoy heaven here and hereafter.

May the Lord bless you.

JD 11:321-330

Made in the USA
Coppell, TX
25 July 2022